Published by Neuron Publishing
www.neuronpublishing.com
www.LoveBookOnline.com

THE BIG ACTIVITY BOOK
for couples!

Thanks for buying the Big Activity Book for couples! If you didn't buy it, but instead received it as a gift, then congrats! If you stole it from your cousin's house because it looked too fun to pass up, then shame on you, but we're flattered that you would go to such lengths. We suggest you buy your cousin another copy though, just for good karma.

We're assuming you bought this book to play the games, but really, you can use it however you like! We think it makes a great coaster for your morning coffee, or it'd make a fantastic therapeutic device - just rip the pages out one by one and kick it around the room. Honestly, we know you'll have fun no matter what, so go for it! (But really, to get the most out of this book you should probably play the games with your partner.)

The Games:

Let the games begin!

You're Awesome At...

EACH OF YOU WILL CUT OR TEAR OUT ONE OF THESE GAME PAGES. WITHOUT LOOKING AT YOUR PARTNERS PAGE, WRITE DOWN ADJECTIVES, NOUNS, VERBS, AND SCENARIOS THAT FIT YOUR PARTNERS AWESOMENESS IN THESE SITUATIONS:

1. Talking people out of _____ .

2. Opening _____ with _____ .

3. Making _____ out of _____ .

4. Wearing _____ confidently, even in _____ places.

5. Inventing _____ out of _____ .

6. Making people _____ .

7. Eating _____ without _____ .

8. Having the uncanny ability to _____ .

9. Convincing people to _____ in their _____ .

10. Preparing for _____ with limited _____ .

11. Redeeming yourself by _____ .

12. Watching _____ while _____ .

13. Maintaining your composure when _____ .

14. _____ like no one is _____ .

15. Being a great _____ .

16. Encouraging others to _____ .

17. _____ while holding a _____ .

18. Making me feel like _____ .

You're Awesome At...

THIS IS JUST THE SECOND PAGE OF THIS GAME, SO NOTHING REALLY NEEDS TO BE WRITTEN HERE. BUT WE JUST WANTED TO SAY HI.

1. Talking people out of _____.

2. Opening _____ with _____.

3. Making _____ out of _____.

4. Wearing _____ confidently, even in _____ places.

5. Inventing _____ out of _____.

6. Making people _____.

7. Eating _____ without _____.

8. Having the uncanny ability to _____.

9. Convincing people to _____ in their _____.

10. Preparing for _____ with limited _____.

11. Redeeming yourself by _____.

12. Watching _____ while _____.

13. Maintaining your composure when _____.

14. _____ like no one is _____.

15. Being a great _____.

16. Encouraging others to _____.

17. _____ while holding a _____.

18. Making me feel like _____.

Versus

Listed below are competing items. Choose which one you each prefer, and write your name on the respective side. Get to know your partner better by comparing and debating your choices!

———————————— Dog or Cat ————————————

———————————— Pepsi or Coke ————————————

———————————— Summer or Winter ————————————

———————————— Night or Day ————————————

———————————— Piercings or Tattoos ————————————

———————————— Milkshakes or Smoothies ————————————

———————————— Paper or E-Books/Audio Books ————————————

———————————— PC or Mac ————————————

———————————— Flying or Driving ————————————

———————————— Fancy or Casual ————————————

———————————— Coffee or Tea ————————————

———————————— Guitar Riff or Drum Solo ————————————

———————————— City or Country ————————————

———————————— Blonde or Brunette ————————————

———————————— Indoors or Outdoors ————————————

———————————— Tropical or Polar ————————————

———————————— Texting or Talking ————————————

———————————— Flowers or Jewelry ————————————

Mini Bucket List

We've put together a list of fun things to do together. Pick the ones you like best and plan out how you'd accomplish them. When you've done it, check it off and write the date accomplished. This is a great way to talk about the goals you want to accomplish together!

☐ Visit a place of personal historical significance. Date: _____

☐ Conquer your biggest fears together. Date: _____

☐ Perform a favor for a stranger. Date: _____

☐ Go on the ultimate romantic getaway. Date: _____

☐ Get on TV; either local or national. Date: _____

☐ Take a road trip. Date: _____

☐ Discover your true passion. Date: _____

☐ Spend a day in someone else's shoes. Date: _____

☐ Volunteer with an organization you believe in. Date: _____

☐ Learn a foreign language. Date: _____

☐ Do one thing that's out of your comfort zone. Date: _____

☐ Design your dream something. Date: _____

☐ Make your dream something a reality. Date: _____

☐ Pick a charitable cause and make a donation. Date: _____

☐ Do something amazing for your family. Date: _____

☐ Accomplish your biggest educational aspiration.   Date: _____

☐ Discover and achieve your spiritual balance.   Date: _____

☐ Do something that's completely spontaneous.   Date: _____

☐ Give back to your community.   Date: _____

☐ Travel in style.   Date: _____

USE THIS SPACE TO COME UP WITH SOME OF YOUR OWN GOALS!

☐ _____   Date: _____

☐ _____   Date: _____

☐ _____   Date: _____

☐ _____   Date: _____

☐ _____   Date: _____

☐ _____   Date: _____

☐ _____   Date: _____

☐ _____   Date: _____

☐ _____   Date: _____

☐ _____   Date: _____

☐ _____   Date: _____

☐ _____   Date: _____

☐ _____   Date: _____

What Would You Be?

CHOOSE A PAGE TO WRITE WHAT YOU THINK YOUR PARTNER WOULD BE IF THEY WERE A TYPE OF THE ITEMS BELOW. DON'T PEEK AT THEIRS! COMPARE ANSWERS TO SEE WHAT YOUR PARTNER THINKS OF YOU.

_____ WOULD BE:

Part of the body: _____

Movie character: _____

TV character: _____

Song: _____

Brand of computer/tech item: _____

Internet browser: _____

Type of tree: _____

Pet: _____

Color of the rainbow: _____

Type of fabric: _____

Hairstyle: _____

Decade: _____

Type of candy: _____

Profession: _____

Personality type: _____

Video game: _____

Historical figure: _____

Type of vehicle: _____

Superhero: _____

Type of food: _____

Type of wine: _____

Type of Plant: _____

An animal: _____

Any country: _____

Musical instrument: _____

Children's toy: _____

An article of clothing: _____

Any flavor of jellybean: _____

Appliance: _____

Sport: _____

Quote: _____

Book: _____

Type of store: _____

Vacation spot: _____

Cartoon: _____

Type of beer: _____

Holiday: _____

Board game: _____

Style of glasses: _____

_____ WOULD BE:

Part of the body: _____

_____

Movie character: _____

_____

TV character: _____

_____

Song: _____

Brand of computer/tech item: _____

Internet browser: _____

Type of tree: _____

Pet: _____

Color of the Rainbow: _____

Type of fabric: _____

Hairstyle: _____

Decade: _____

Type of candy: _____

Profession: _____

Personality type: _____

Video game: _____

Historical figure: _____

Type of vehicle: _____

SupeRheRo: _____

Type of food: _____

Type of Wine: _____

Type of Plant: _____

An animal: _____

Any countRy: _____

Musical instRument: _____

ChildRen's toy: _____

An aRticle of clothing: _____

Any flavoR of jellybean: _____

Appliance: _____

SpoRt: _____

Quote: _____

Book: _____

Type of stoRe: _____

Vacation spot: _____

CaRtoon: _____

Type of beeR: _____

Holiday: _____

BoaRd game: _____

Style of glasses: _____

Keep the Convo Going

Set a timer for 60 seconds. One of you will start the conversation with a statement or question. Your partner must respond with a relevant statement or question in which the first word starts with the last letter of the previous sentence. The last person to think of a relevant sentence before time is up wins! (Ex. Person 1: "What should we do today?" Person 2: "You know, a picnic might be nice!" Person 1: "Especially in this weather!"...). Here are some starter ideas:

1. Talk about what you'd like to do on a rainy day.

2. Tell each other your thoughts on a recent movie you've seen.

3. Dream about your future plans.

4. Reminisce about the last holiday you spent together.

5. Discuss what technological advancement has made the biggest impact on society in the last ten years.

6. Debate the best way to make pancakes.

Some variations:

- Only speak in questions.

- Start each sentence in alphabetical order. (Person one's first letter starts with A, Person two's first letter starts with B...)

- Use a one word subject for the whole time (such as breakfast, celebrities, creatures, etc.)

Beat The Noun

ONE OF YOU STARTS BY WRITING DOWN A NOUN, RELEVANT TO THE THEMES BELOW, IN THE GIVEN SPACE. NEXT TO IT, YOUR PARTNER WILL WRITE ANOTHER NOUN THAT MAY "BEAT" YOUR NOUN. YOU'LL THEN READ THE NOUNS ALOUD, RESULTING IN RIDICULOUS DEBATES OVER WHETHER A NOUN, IN FACT, BEATS ANOTHER NOUN! (EX. DOES JACK BAUER BEAT CHUCK NORRIS? OF COURSE HE DOESN'T. NO ONE BEATS CHUCK NORRIS.)

Movie Characters: _____ _____

TV characters: _____ _____

Food & Drink: _____ _____

Music: _____ _____

Technology: _____ _____

Game Shows/Hosts: _____ _____

Celebrities: _____ _____

Wild Animals: _____ _____

Books: _____ _____

Travel Destinations: _____ _____

Reality Shows: _____ _____

Countries: _____ _____

Historical Figures: _____ _____

Types of Monsters: _____ _____

Fictional Heroes: _____ _____

Fictional Villains: _____ _____

The Maze Race

First, each of you should choose a maze. Before starting the game, write down three rewards you want the other person to fulfill for you (ex. buy me a flatscreen TV; take me to a taping of my favorite game show, etc). Take turns completing your mazes. Each time you hit a dead-end, your partner can choose one reward from their list! Three dead-ends is the max. If you get through the maze without any errors, you get to choose a reward from your partner! Psych them out during their gameplay to rack up more rewards!

START HERE

END HERE

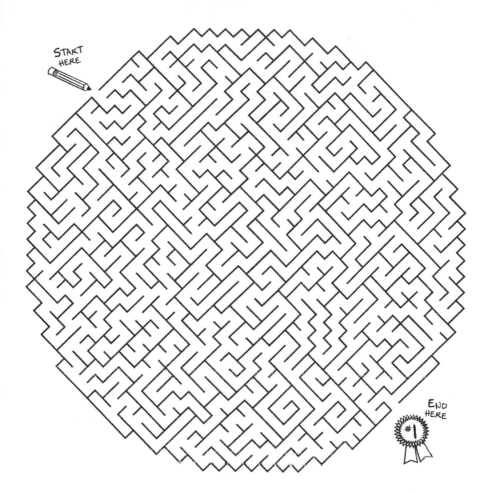

START
HERE

END
HERE

Write your Rewards here:

Player 1:

1.

2.

3.

Player 2:

1.

2.

3.

Movie Mash-Up

EACH OF YOU PICK YOUR FAVORITE MOVIE GENRE. TOGETHER, WRITE A MOVIE BASED ON BOTH GENRES. (EX: ROMANTIC COMEDY & ACTION) YOU'LL EACH WRITE ONE CHAPTER IN THE TONE OF YOUR CHOSEN GENRE, THEN PASS IT TO YOUR PARTNER TO WRITE ANOTHER CHAPTER, SO ON AND SO FORTH. MAKE IT EVEN FUNNIER BY SWAPPING AFTER EACH PARAGRAPH!

GenRe 1: _____   GenRe 2: _____

Title: _____

_____

_____

_____

_____

_____

_____

_____

_____

_____

_____

_____

_____

_____

_____

_____

_____

_____

_____

_____

_____

_____

_____

_____

_____

_____

_____

_____

_____

_____

_____

_____

_____

_____

_____

_____

_____

_____

_____

_____

_____

_____

_____

_____

_____

_____

The End!

The Newlywed-ish Game

GRAB YOUR SPOUSE, PARTNER, OR THAT PERSON YOU JUST MET AT A COFFEE SHOP AND WORK TOGETHER TO COME UP WITH A LIST OF QUESTIONS TO ASK EACH OTHER. YOU WILL WRITE AN ANSWER ABOUT YOUR PARTNER, THEN ABOUT YOURSELF. (EX. WHAT'S MY FAVORITE COLOR? YOU'LL WRITE DOWN WHAT YOU THINK THEIRS IS, AND WHAT YOURS IS). CHOOSE A PAGE TO WRITE YOUR ANSWERS ON, AND RIP IT OUT OF THE BOOK. MAKE SURE YOUR PARTNER DOESN'T LOOK AT YOUR ANSWERS! ALTERNATE ASKING EACH OTHER QUESTIONS, AND COMPARE THEIR ANSWERS WITH YOURS TO SEE HOW WELL THEY KNOW YOU!

Question 1: _____

Question 2: _____

Question 3: _____

Question 4: _____

Question 5: _____

Question 6: _____

Question 7: _____

Question 8: _____

Question 9: _____

Question 10: _____

Question 11: _____

Question 12: _____

Question 13: _____

Question 14: _____

Question 15: _____

_____ , SAYS:

Answer 1: Them – _____ Me –_____

Answer 2: Them – _____ Me –_____

Answer 3: Them – _____ Me –_____

Answer 4: Them – _____ Me –_____

Answer 5: Them – _____ Me –_____

Answer 6: Them – _____ Me –_____

Answer 7: Them – _____ Me –_____

Answer 8: Them – _____ Me –_____

Answer 9: Them – _____ Me –_____

Answer 10: Them – _____ Me –_____

Answer 11: Them – _____ Me –_____

Answer 12: Them – _____ Me –_____

Answer 13: Them – _____ Me –_____

Answer 14: Them – _____ Me –_____

Answer 15: Them – _____ Me –_____

_____ , SAYS:

Answer 1: Them - _____ Me -_____

Answer 2: Them - _____ Me -_____

Answer 3: Them - _____ Me -_____

Answer 4: Them - _____ Me -_____

Answer 5: Them - _____ Me -_____

Answer 6: Them - _____ Me -_____

Answer 7: Them - _____ Me -_____

Answer 8: Them - _____ Me -_____

Answer 9: Them - _____ Me -_____

Answer 10: Them - _____ Me -_____

Answer 11: Them - _____ Me -_____

Answer 12: Them - _____ Me -_____

Answer 13: Them - _____ Me -_____

Answer 14: Them - _____ Me -_____

Answer 15: Them - _____ Me -_____

What's Their Story?

The next time you're out in a public place and have some free time, point out a random person and ask the your partner to imagine what they are thinking, how are they feeling, etc. You may also ask where they work, if they are happy, as well as any other questions. Swap turns after the story is done. You can come up with some pretty hilarious stories! After the game is over, decide who came up with the best story and reward that person with ice cream, a coffee, or just a little smooch!

Would You Rather?

PLAY A QUICK GAME OF ROCK, PAPER, SCISSORS TO DETERMINE WHO WILL BE PLAYER 1 (OBVIOUSLY, THE WINNER WILL BE PLAYER 1). ANSWER THE QUESTIONS BELOW, AND EXPLAIN YOUR REASONING TO MAKE THE GAME MORE INTERESTING!

Travel by air or by sea?

1._____ 2._____

Star in a music video or a reality TV show?

1._____ 2._____

Be President or a King/Queen?

1._____ 2._____

Live alone in a mansion or with 8 people in 3 bedroom house?

1._____ 2._____

Loan a friend money (that you know you will never be paid back) or donate that same amount to a charity?

1._____ 2._____

Have the power to change one existing law or have the power to make one new law?

1._____ 2._____

Have infinite knowledge or infinite power?

1._____ 2._____

Be book smart or street smart?

1._____ 2._____

Speak to a huge crowd or hold a snake?

1._____ 2._____

Have to fire someone or be fired?

1._____ 2._____

Be 10 pounds thinner or have an IQ that is 10 points higher?

1._____ 2._____

Vacation at a tropical hotel or at a wooded mountain cabin?

1._____ 2._____

Always know what time it is without a clock or always know
where you are without a map?

1._____ 2._____

Go a year without sugar or a year without salt?

1._____ 2._____

Be the driver or the passenger?

1._____ 2._____

Lose your sight or your hearing?

1._____ 2._____

Be drop-dead gorgeous or hilariously funny?

1._____ 2._____

Be the smartest person in the world, or the best-looking perons in the world?

1._____ 2._____

Be served breakfast in bed or go out to a romantic dinner?

1._____ 2._____

Eat an appetizer or a dessert?

1._____ 2._____

ON THESE NEXT FEW, FILL IN THE BLANKS WITH YOUR OQN SCENARIOS!

Go backstage with _____ or go on tour with _____?

Meet _____ or go on a date with _____?

Spend a day as _____ or a week as _____?

Watch a 24 hour _____ marathon, or hang out with the

cast of _____ for a day?

Two Truths and a Lie

Tear out the next two pages and separately write three statements— two true and one false— about your life or experiences for each round of gameplay. Also, write down a reward for yourself if you win two out of three rounds. Don't show your partner your page! One of you will read your statements aloud, and the other will question you for further details about them. You must tell the truth about the two true ones, but you can lie to conceal the false one. Your partner has two choices to guess which one is the lie. He/She gets two points for choosing the correct lie on the first try; and one for choosing it on the second. Switch roles, and tally your points below.

Round:	_____ 's points:	_____ 's points:
One		
Two		
Three		

In the event of a tie, here is a quick tiebreaker game:

Whoever's birthday is closest to today's date wins!
(If you have the same birthday, you're on your own in deciding who won!)

_____ 's Truths and Lies:

Round One:

1. _____

2. _____

3. _____

Round Two:

1. _____

2. _____

3. _____

Round Three:

1. _____

2. _____

3. _____

My reward for winning: _____

_____

_____ 's Truths and Lies:

Round One:

1. _____

2. _____

3. _____

Round Two:

1. _____

2. _____

3. _____

Round Three:

1. _____

2. _____

3. _____

My reward for winning: _____

_____

Do You Know Me?

Together, randomly decide on twenty questions out of the list below to ask each other. If your partner answers correctly (you'll be the judge), he or she receives the number of points indicated for that question, and you receive one point. If your partner answers incorrectly, neither of you receives any points. The same rules apply when you answer. The winner is the person with the higher score after you've both answered all twenty questions! There are 60 questions, so you can play a few times!

☐ Name my two closest friends..................................2 pts

☐ What is my favorite musical group or composer?...........2 pts

☐ What was I wearing when we first met?......................2 pts

☐ Name one of my hobbies....................................3 pts

☐ Where was I born?..1 pt

☐ What stresses am I facing right now?........................4 pts

☐ Describe in detail what I did today, or yesterday...........4 pts

- [ ] When is my birthday?...1 pt
- [ ] What is the date of our anniversary?...................................1 pt
- [ ] Who is my favorite relative?..2 pts
- [ ] What is my fondest unrealized dream?...............................5 pts
- [ ] What is my favorite flower?..2 pts
- [ ] What is one of my greatest fears?...................................3 pts
- [ ] What is my favorite time of day for being romantic?......3 pts
- [ ] What makes me feel most competent?...........................4 pts
- [ ] What are my turn-ons?...3 pts
- [ ] What is my favorite meal?..2 pts
- [ ] What is my favorite way to spend an evening?................2 pts
- [ ] What is my favorite color?..1 pt
- [ ] What improvements do I want to make in my life?...........4 pts
- [ ] What kind of present would I like best?.......................2pts
- [ ] What was one of my best childhood experiences?.............2 pts
- [ ] What was my favorite vacation?...................................2 pts
- [ ] What is one of my favorite ways to be soothed?.............4 pts
- [ ] Who is my best source of support (other than you)?.......3 pts

- [ ] What is my favorite sport?.................................2 pts
- [ ] What do I most like to do with time off?..................2
- [ ] pts
- [ ] What is one of my favorite weekend activities?.............2 pts
- [ ] What is my favorite getaway place?.......................2 pts
- [ ] What is my favorite movie?...............................2 pts
- [ ] What is one important event coming up in my life?.........4 pts
- [ ] What are some of my favorite ways to work out?...........2 pts
- [ ] Who was my best friend in childhood?....................3 pts
- [ ] What is one of my favorite magazines?....................2 pts
- [ ] Name one of my major rivals or "enemies."................3 pts
- [ ] What would I consider my ideal job?......................4 pts
- [ ] What do I fear the most?................................4 pts
- [ ] Who is my least favorite relative?.......................4 pts
- [ ] What is my favorite holiday?............................2 pts
- [ ] What kinds of books do I most like to read?..............3 pts
- [ ] What is my favorite TV show?............................2 pts
- [ ] Which side of the bed do I prefer?.......................2 pts

- [ ] What am I most sad about?..............................4 pts

- [ ] Name one of my concerns or worries..........................4 pts

- [ ] What medical problems do I worry about?....................2 pts

- [ ] What was my most embarrassing moment?....................3 pts

- [ ] What was my worst childhood experience?....................3 pts

- [ ] Name two of the people I most admire..........................4 pts

- [ ] Name my major rival or enemy..........................3 pts

- [ ] Who is my least favorite person?..........................3 pts

- [ ] What is one of my favorite desserts?..........................2 pts

- [ ] What is my social security number?..........................2 pts

- [ ] Name one of my favorite novels..........................2 pts

- [ ] What is my favorite restaurant?..........................2 pts

- [ ] What are two of my aspirations, hopes, wishes?..............4 pts

- [ ] Do I have a secret ambition? What is it?..........................4 pts

- [ ] What foods do I hate?..........................2 pts

- [ ] What is my favorite animal?..........................2 pts

- [ ] What is my favorite song?..........................2 pts

- [ ] Which sports team is my favorite?..........................2 pts

Draw It or Act It

Grab a few sheets of paper to draw and write on. Each of you should write down items that fit the themes below, but keep them secret from your partner! These will be the items you draw or act out. Use a timer set for 60 seconds and, taking turns, randomly choose an item from your list while your partner guesses what you're drawing or acting out. Do not tell them the theme, unless they need a hint. Give one point for each correct answer. Rules: You can't write words or numbers, no saying "rhymes with", no table talk!

- Something that reminds you of your first date

- One of your favorite foods

- A scene from your favorite movie/TV show

- Your favorite attribute about your partner

- Your "pet" names for each other

- Your favorite holiday memory

- Something fun you did together on vacation

- One of your combined goals or dreams

- The best gift your partner gave you

- Something your partner loves about you

- The cutest thing your sweetie does subconsciously

- One of your hobbies

- Your most embarrassing moment

- Your dream profession

Your Favorite Restaurant

DRAW YOUR FAVORITE RESTAURANT MEMORY YOU SHARED DURING A NIGHT OUT.

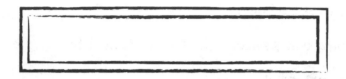

All About Them

Decide who will be Player One and who will be Player Two. Using your own pages, write about your favorite memories with your sweetie, things you love about them, etc. This makes such a great keepsake, we suggest framing it to hang on your wall.

Player One, aka _____ , says:

Three reasons why I love you are: _____

_____

Your biggest pet peeve is: _____

One thing you think is a flaw in yourself, but I find adorable is:

_____

Movies that remind me of you are: _____

_____

Activities I love doing with you are: _____

_____

The first thing I noticed about you was: _____

_____

The color you look best in is: _____

When we hold hands, I feel: _____

_____

My favorite thing about your family/friends is: _____

_____

I love that your greatest talents are: _____

_____

Our first kiss was: _____

_____

My favorite way of communicating with you is: _____

_____

The best gift you ever got me was: _____

_____

Your three best features (in my eyes) are: _____

_____

Three adjectives that best describe you are: _____

_____

I love when you: _____

_____

Three adjectives that best describe our relationship are:

_____

_____

My favorite time with you has been: _____

_____

Songs that remind me of you are: _____

_____

The most adorable thing about you is: _____

_____

An activity I love watching you do is: _____

_____

My favorite thing to do with you is: _____

_____

Our funniest memory is: _____

_____

Our most embarassing moment together was: _____

_____

A few quotes that remind me of you are: _____

_____

_____

_____

_____

All About Them

Player Two, aka ___Sean___ , says:

Three reasons why I love you are: ___ass, tits,___
___hairy labias___

Your biggest pet peeve is: ___when you speak___

One thing you think is a flaw in yourself, but I find adorable is:
___your attitude___

Movies that remind me of you are: ___Bikini Pirates___

Activities I love doing with you are: ___sex (in bed,___
___hotel shower) and eating (food + ass)___

The first thing I noticed about you was: ___big butt___

The color you look best in is: ___everything___

When we hold hands, I feel: ___sweat___

My favorite thing about your family/friends is: _they like me more_

I love that your greatest talents are: _getting me hard_

Our first kiss was: _sad_

My favorite way of communicating with you is: _yelling sexual things_

The best gift you ever got me was: _blowjob_

Your three best features (in my eyes) are: _ass, tits, slappable butt cheeks_

Three adjectives that best describe you are: _bodacious, beautiful, bangable_

I love when you: _were doing sex_

Three adjectives that best describe our relationship are: _sad, sexy, subtle_

My favorite time with you has been: ___first bj___

Songs that remind me of you are: ___I Touch Myself___

The most adorable thing about you is: ___your butt___

An activity I love watching you do is: ___reverse cowgirl___

My favorite thing to do with you is: ___sex___

Our funniest memory is: ___When I made your
tits fart during sex___

Our most embarassing moment together was: ___When I had
diarrhea after Benihana___

A few quotes that remind me of you are: _____
___"I love anal"___
___"Let's fuck!"___
___"You look so sexy"___

The Matching Game

Based on what you think of your honey's body, match the body parts on the left with the adjective that best describes it on the right. Write in your own body part ideas in the blanks!

What _____ thinks of _____ :

Back	Sexy
Neck	Hairy
Legs	Cute
Arms	Adorable
Belly	Masculine
Chest	Feminine
Feet	Soft
Hands	Hard
Fingers	Gorgeous
Toes	Beautiful
Hair	Big
Eyes	Small
Butt	Curvy
Ears	Muscular
Mouth	Sweet
Lips	Stunning
Nose	Dainty
PENIS	Firm
BUTT	Strong
BUTT	Handsome
	Pretty
	Graceful

53

The Matching Game

What _____ thinks of _____ :

Back	Sexy
Neck	Hairy
Legs	Cute
Arms	Adorable
Belly	Masculine
Chest	Feminine
Feet	Soft
Hands	Hard
Fingers	Gorgeous
Toes	Beautiful
Hair	Big
Eyes	Small
Butt	Curvy
Ears	Muscular
Mouth	Sweet
Lips	Stunning
Nose	Dainty
_____	Firm
_____	Strong
_____	Handsome
	Pretty
	Graceful

Rate the Traits

Rate these partner personality traits in order of importance to you. Write your numbers, 1-20 with 1 being most important, in a respective column. Trade answers to get to know each other better!

___ ___	Trustworthiness		___ ___	Respect
___ ___	Honesty		___ ___	Intelligence
___ ___	Sense of Humor		___ ___	Non-Judgemental
___ ___	Sexiness		___ ___	Similar Interests
___ ___	Selflessness		___ ___	Active
___ ___	Caring		___ ___	Responsible
___ ___	Thoughtfulness		___ ___	Supportive
___ ___	Sympathy		___ ___	Confident
___ ___	Kindness			
___ ___	Understanding			
___ ___	Appreciative			
___ ___	Intimacy			

Let's Travel!

Label the places you've been together, and mark any places you'd like to visit in the future!

DRess Me Up

On the stick figure, draw the style that you like most on your better half.
Think clothing, hairstyles, accessories, etc. Get creative!

DRess Me Up

On the stick figure, draw the style that you like most on your better half.
Think clohting, hairstyles, accessories, etc. Get creative!

Our Favorite Things

On these next two blank pages, work together to write, draw, or paste pictures of what you two decide are your most valued things in life. You can come up with existing items, future dreams, or shared interests. Turn it into your own inspiration board!

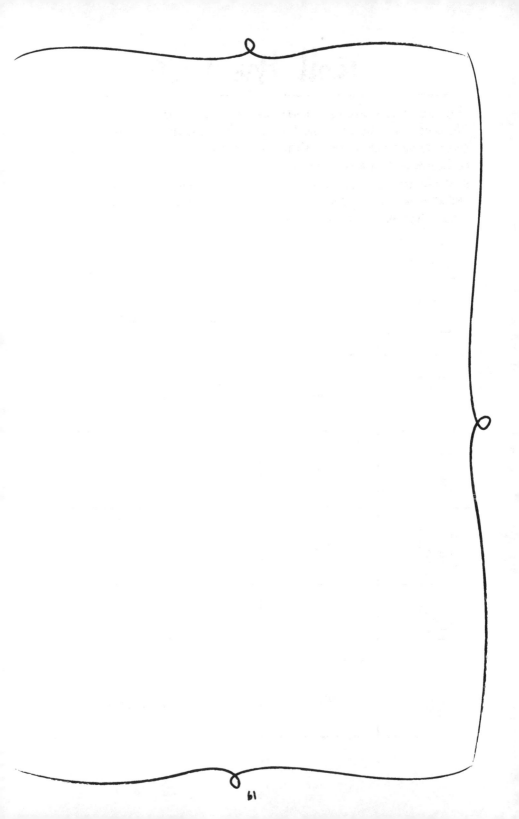

Roll the Dice

FOR THIS GAME YOU'LL NEED A PAIR OF DICE. DESIGNATE ONE DIE AS "ACTIONS" AND THE OTHER AS "PLACES". YOU CAN MARK ONE WITH A COLOR TO DISTINGUISH THEM. NOTICE BELOW THAT EACH ACTION AND PLACE CORRESPONDS WITH A NUMBER ON THE DICE. ROLL THE DIE, AND SEE WHAT NUMBERS YOU GET. (EX. YOU ROLL A 1 AND A 5. THAT MEANS YOU HAVE TO EAT AT YOUR FAVORITE COFFEE SHOP!) HAVE FUN DOING THE ACTIONS IN THE PLACES THEY MATCH UP WITH!

DIE SIDES:	ACTIONS:	PLACES:
⚀	EAT	OUR FAVORITE RESTAURANT
⚁	DRINK	OUR FAVORITE PARK
⚂	PLAY	OUR LIVING ROOM
⚃	RUN	OUR KITCHEN
⚄	LAUGH	OUR FAVORITE COFFEE SHOP
⚅	TALK	OUR PATIO/PORCH/BALCONY

Remember for Rewards!

Cut out the cards on this page and the next, then lay them face down in a grid pattern on the floor or a table. One person will flip two cards over. If you match the two cards, you get whatever is written on it from your partner and you get another turn! If you don't match them, flip them back over. Your partner now has a turn. Gameplay continues this way until all the cards have been flipped and matched. Make up your own cards for even more fun!

Back Massage	Back Massage
Foot Rub	Foot Rub
Candlelight Dinner	Candlelight Dinner
Breakfast in Bed	Breakfast in Bed
One Date Night (my choice)	One Date Night (my choice)

One "free" Day (to do whatever I want)	One "free" Day (to do whatever I want)
Control of the TV (for one night)	Control of the TV (for one night)
Surprise Gift (hand-made or store bought)	Surprise Gift (hand-made or store bought)
Movie Night (my choice)	Movie Night (my choice)
Do chores for a Day (my choice)	Do chores for a Day (my choice)
Clean my Car	Clean my Car
Wild Card (I decide the reward!)	Wild Card (I decide the reward!)

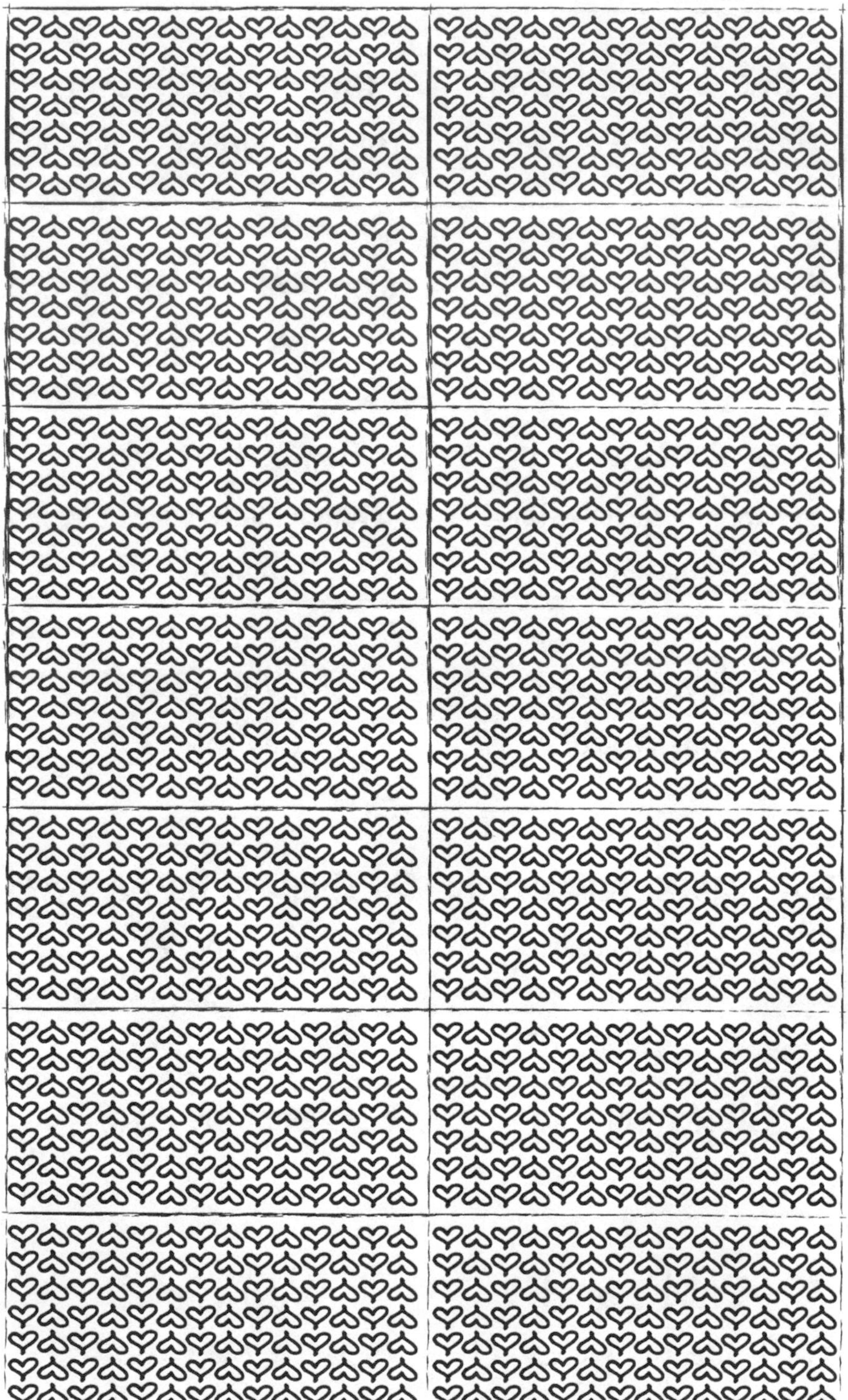

Scavenger Hunts

These games take a little time and effort, but will end up being so fun! You can be creative with the ideas we list below, plus have fun making up your own!

1. Using candy, place a trail from the entryway of your home to wherever you want your partner to end up, then place a prize at that location!

2. Make riddle cards and place the first one where your love will see it upon coming home. Create a clue that will lead them to the next card or location, and so on. You can even hide the cards in public places, and make up clues to lead them on an outdoor adventure! (For example, "Go to the first coffee shop we dated at); stuff like that. At the end have a surprise, maybe like a pre-planned date, waiting!

3. Make a scavenger hunt that requires little movement! Challenge your partner to answer pre-made questions regarding your relationship (whether past or present events, qualities or activities), and keep score on how many answers are dead-on or close to the actual event. Have small rewards to give for each answer, or chose a big present for the entire game!

4. Make up a scavenger hunt together! Come up with the theme, how you'll create the puzzles, and if you'll work together or separate.

Love Libs

Ask your partner for words to fill in the blanks and create an adorably funny story to share with each other!

CARNIVAL DATE

For our __15__ year anniversary, __Sean__ Little butt
NUMBER   SIGNIFICANT OTHER

and I decided to go to the carnival in town. We both love the

atmosphere- the smells, sights, and sounds get us so __Sticky__!
ADJECTIVE

The first thing we did was eat. We each devoured some elephant

__ball sacks__ and __hydrangeas__ candy. No carnival
BODY PART - PLURAL   TYPE OF PLANT

meal is complete without some freshly-squeezed __yellow semen__.
LIQUID

Next, we played our favorite carnival games. We won a stuffed

__toot__ by popping balloons with __light sabers__. I won a
NOUN   WEAPON - PLURAL

pet __giraffe__ by bouncing a __scrotum__ into a fish bowl.
ANIMAL   TYPE OF BALL

Neither of us had much luck in the __mailbx__ -toss though.
OBJECT

We rode our favorite rides, like bumper __Pope mobile__,
VEHICLE

__slurp__-A-Whirl, and the Ferris Wheel. We even
VERB

shared a(n) __sweaty__ kiss in the
ADJECTIVE

Tunnel of __horny__.
EMOTION

__Tequila kelly__ and I decided to get our fortunes read
SIGNIFICANT OTHER

by the __bodacious__ psychic. She told us that we were
ADJECTIVE

__floppy__ and very happy about it. She also predicted
ADJECTIVE

we'd have __22__ kids and live in __jail__.
NUMBER .... A PLACE

Finally, we got the courage to go through the __Stench-tacular__
ADJECTIVE

house. I screamed, "__SHIT NIGGERS+CUNT FLAPS__" when
EXCLAMATION

the __DILDO__ jumped out at us! It really scared the
OBJECT

__areolas__ out of us both! What a fun date!
NOUN

Love Libs

ROMANTIC GETAWAY

For our first _sweaty_ (ADJECTIVE) getaway, We decided

to travel by _pink vomit_ (NOUN) to our dream vacation spot in

kellys anus (A PLACE). We planned for _seconds_ (UNIT OF TIME - PLURAL) to be

sure the vacation was _lubricated_ (ADJECTIVE). After traveling for

_72_ (A NUMBER) hours, we finally arrived at _Grandmas house_ (PLACE)

and immediately checked in. Our Room was positively, absolutely

unrelenting (ADJECTIVE)! We decided to head down to the

pocket pussy (NOUN) to enjoy a _tight_ (ADJECTIVE) lunch. As the sun set,

we took a relaxing _thrust_ (VERB) on the _Ollie's tight anus_ (NOUN)

Holding _scrotums_ (BODY PART - PLURAL), we felt so _contageous_ (AN EMOTION) to be alone

together. We stayed way past sunset, watching the _condums_ (NOUN - PLURAL)

and _veins_ (NOUN - PLURAL) doing _fart_ (VERB). The rest of our

vacation was spent doing _Pillage_ (ACTIVITY) and _sex_ (ACTIVITY).

After _2_ (A NUMBER) days of relaxation, we headed home. Overall, it

was the most _sexy mama_ (ADJECTIVE) vacation ever!

70

Love Libs

ROAD TRIP

One day, I surprised my _____ with a Road
TERM OF ENDEARMENT

trip. With no destination in mind, we _____
VERB - PAST TENSE

into the car and _____ away. First, we
VERB - PAST TENSE

stopped at a _____ for snacks and to fill up with
TYPE OF BUILDING

_____. By _____ o'clock we were on our
NOUN - PLURAL   A NUMBER

way! We drove through the _____ forests and
ADJECTIVE

_____ mountains. We held _____
ADJECTIVE   BODY PART - PLURAL

while listening to our favorite song, _____
NAME OF A SONG

on the Radio. The scenery was so _____ ,
ADJECTIVE

we pulled out the _____ and took pictures. On our
NOUN

way home, we found a _____ Restaurant to stop
ADJECTIVE

at and _____. After _____ we finally made it
VERB   A TIME

home. I have to say, it was the most _____
ADJECTIVE

trip we've ever taken together!

Love Libs

VACATION ADVENTURE

It all started with our adventure vacation in
<u>a nude beach</u>. It was just me and <u>Flappy Butt Kelly</u>

VACATION SPOT   SIGNIFICANT OTHER

- we were excited to just be out of the <u>Ollyantatambo</u>

CITY

rat race. On day one we wanted to relax by the pool. With a
<u>horse piss</u> in one hand and <u>douche bags</u> in the

BEVERAGE   NOUN

other, we knew this vacation would be like no other.

As we soaked up the sun, the DJ started playing my favorite

song, <u>I Touch Myself</u>! I was so excited I couldn't help but yell,

SONG TITLE

"<u>fuck me in the ars</u>!" and jump into the pool.

EXCLAMATION

Unfortunately, I had not waited an hour before swimming and all

those <u>chicken vags</u> were starting to cause a cramp. I was

FOOD — PLURAL

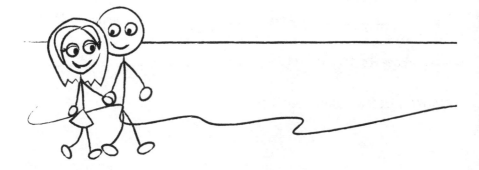

sinking fast. No matter how much I __jacked off__ ,
_{VERB - PAST TENSE}
I couldn't stay afloat.

I felt someone grab my __beefy labias__ but somehow slipped
_{BODY PART}
free. It turns out that it was the __pimp__ at the
_{JOB TITLE}
hotel, who looked a lot like __Ron Jeremy__ . Just then,
_{CELEBRITY}
__awkward Sean__ tied a __strap on__ to a __door knob__ and
_{SIGNIFICANT OTHER} _{NOUN} _{NOUN}
tossed it in the pool. You wouldn't think that it would float, but

it did the job! I grabbed a hold and was pulled out of the water.

Once out of the pool, I dried off using a(n) __crusty__
_{ADJECTIVE}
__poop__ . I thanked my hero with a big kiss on the
_{NOUN}
__anus__ and we enjoyed the rest of our vacation!
_{BODY PART}

Top Ten

Circle the top ten adjectives that you love about your partner! Use two different colored pens so you can compare afterward.

Gentle   Trustworthy   Energetic

Sexy   Sympathetic   Calm

    Outgoing   Silly

Honest   Kind   Goofy   Sensitive

    Cheerful   Loving   Intelligent

Humorous   Appreciative   Likable

Creative   Exotic   Courageous   Friendly

        Understanding   Passionate

Good Looking   Flexible   Feisty   Adventurous

        Responsible

Caring   Selfless   Loyal   Muscular

    Grateful   Accommodating   Comfortable

Active   Beautiful   Sincere   Handsome

    Thoughtful

Intimate   Supportive   Cooperative

        Confident

        Devoted   Sweet   Easy-Going

            Fun

    Non-Judgemental   Romantic

                Classy

        Respectful

OuR FavoRite TV Show

DRAW THE SHOW THAT YOU AND YOUR HONEY LOVE TO SNUGGLE TO ON THE SCREEN. IF YOU CAN'T DRAW WELL, JUST WRITE THE NAMES. LOOK BACK LATER TO SEE IF YOUR TASTES HAVE CHANGED!

Your Favorite Holiday

CHOOSE YOUR SIGNIFICANT OTHER'S FAVORITE HOLIDAY(S). WRITE A MEMORABLE STORY OR ANECDOTE TO READ LATER AND REMINISCE ABOUT!

Christmas	Halloween	Independence Day
New Years	Hanukkah	Mother's Day
Valentine's Day	Rosh Hashanah	Father's Day
St. Patrick's Day	Yom Kippur	Ramadan
Labor Day	Kwanzza	Chinese New Year
Memorial Day	Mardi Gras	Martin Luther King Day
Thanksgiving	April Fool's Day	Passover
Easter	Cinco De Mayo	Purim

Your Favorite Holiday

Choose your significant other's favorite holiday(s). Write a memorable story or anecdote to read later and reminisce about!

Christmas	Halloween	Independence Day
New Years	Hanukkah	Mother's Day
Valentine's Day	Rosh Hashanah	Father's Day
St. Patrick's Day	Yom Kippur	Ramadan
Labor Day	Kwanzza	Chinese New Year
Memorial Day	Mardi Gras	Martin Luther King Day
Thanksgiving	April Fool's Day	Passover
Easter	Cinco De Mayo	Purim

Facial Expressions

Listed under each head is an emotion. Draw the facial expression that your honey-pie makes when they are experiencing that emotion. Don't enjoy drawing? Paste a photo instead! Player one, use this page.

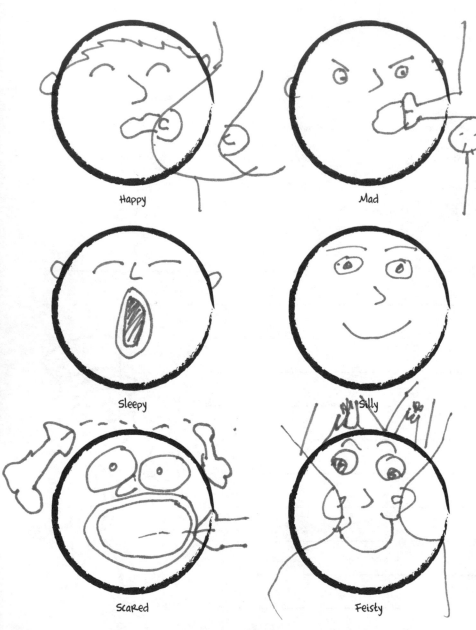

Happy

Mad

Sleepy

Silly

Scared

Feisty

Facial Expressions

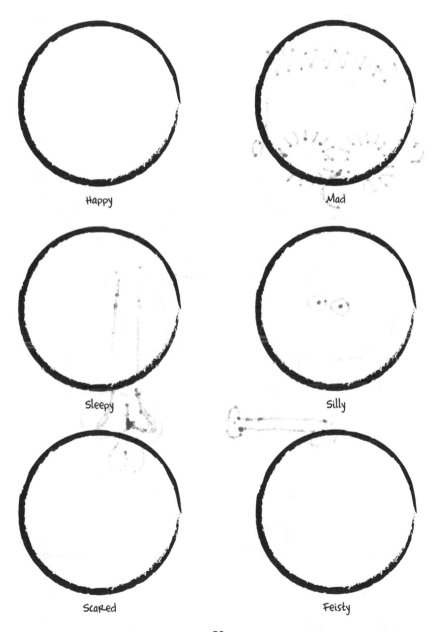

Happy

Mad

Sleepy

Silly

Scared

Feisty

Favorite Body Part

ON THE STICK FIGURES, CIRCLE THE BODY PART (OR PARTS) THAT YOU FIND MOST ATTRACTIVE, SEXY, OR JUST ADORABLE ON YOUR PARTNER!

Front   Back

Favorite Body Part

ON THE STICK FIGURES, CIRCLE THE BODY PART (OR PARTS) THAT YOU FIND MOST ATTRACTIVE, SEXY, OR JUST ADORABLE ON YOUR PARTNER!

Front   Back

Hearts & Squares

BELOW IS A GRID OF HEARTS. ONE OF YOU WILL DRAW A LINE CONNECTING TWO ADJACENT HEARTS. THE OTHER WILL THEN DRAW ANOTHER LINE TO CONNECT ANOTHER TWO HEARTS. THE GOAL IS TO BE THE PERSON WHO DRAWS THE LAST SIDE OF A SQUARE. ONCE YOU COMPLETE A SQUARE, PUT YOUR INITIALS INSIDE OF IT. THE PLAYER WITH THE MOST SQUARES WHEN ALL THE SQUARES ARE DRAWN WINS!

Categories

The grid below lists items on the left and letters on the top. Work together to come up with answers that fit your Dream Items in each category and that start with the letter on the top. (Ex. For the letter V, you might have Venice for a travel destination).

	L	O	V	E
Vehicle				
Travel				
Boy's Names				
Girl's Names				
Goals				
Home				

Sprouting Love

Decide who will go first. Player one, you'll start by drawing a line between any two dots, then draw another dot in the middle of the line you just made. Your partner will then draw a line between any two dots, and put a dot in the middle of that line. Continue taking turns drawing your lines and dots. No lines may cross each other, but they can loop around other lines. Only three lines in total can emerge from any one dot. The dots put in the middle of the lines already have two lines connecting them to the two other dots, so they can only have one more line. The game continues until no more lines can be drawn. The person who draws the last line is the winner!

Word Search

Listed below are words that most likely describe you and your partner. Work together to find them in the puzzle to the right!

Hint: The words may be horizontal, diagonal, and vertical, but will not be written backwards.

☐ Adventurous   ☐ Devoted   ☐ Handsome

☐ Beautiful   ☐ Energetic   ☐ Honest

☐ Calming   ☐ Faithful   ☐ Intelligent

☐ Caring   ☐ Friendly   ☐ Lovely

☐ Cheerful   ☐ Funny   ☐ Selfless

☐ Courageous   ☐ Generous   ☐ Sexy

☐ Creative   ☐ Goofy   ☐ Sincere

    ☐ Smart

    ☐ Sweet

    ☐ Thoughtful

(Answers on page 120)

N Z B F J C Y F L A L A G D P H A T Y

H N E S T E N E R G E L I C D R V O S P V

J N A J J L T N P B A H H K B Q R E X L Y

E E G V U J U X N A E W B N I K B D X L W U

W H M S E H Q G X G M E S Q S V C X G T F

I N E I T N U W L I X S W O W H K J T

O G M Y O I S C A G T L E L M V E W W G H

W M O X V A U C X D I U E L X S W T L O U

E D S O E F O R U L P F E X S M T L O U H

I D P D E B O E N I L E T Z E M T Y

U F N S Q C G W B A A T E N L N E V L T

F L A C M F A C V T J U S M A E I B D S

R K H U C A R I N G N A T H W B C G N J

E K O X L R U Q X Y A E C S K R U Q E E

E Q L D D H O P H Y S B J L F E P U S

H E Y J N F N C K G O Y P B C T Z E U F R C

C E S A D V E G T U R B O U S V R N F L

R R A H C M T V G E W G B S I W H O C M F I

F E C P A J W C M R B B S E U Z T M R H C U M H

Y N C U Q V U L M A R T B V G C C S N Z T M O O F Y C M M

U Z I I Q I L S M V G E N E R O U S W O F M T

G U V N X U Y L S K V O R F E C V K L E W N Z F

M S H J H J I L U C C I L D D S H W J K Q

G M Q K F V O B A U B I M Z K K H I R N

87

Truth or Dare

Choose a truth or a dare. If you choose truth, you have to be honest. If you chose dare, you have to follow through with it!

Truths:

- What's your guilty pleasure movie?

- When you were a kid, what did you think you would be when you grew up?

- What's your favorite thing to do when no one else is home?

- Who irritates you the most?

- What's your worst habit?

- If you could date any celebrity, who would it be?

- What's the funniest thing that you've seen happen, but no one else was around to see?

- What was the worst thing you did as a kid that no one found out about?

- How far would you go to help someone in need?

- How much money would it take for you to quit your job?

- If you could be anyone for a day, who would it be and why?

- If you had the power to change one event in history, which would it be and why?

Dares:

- Put an ice cube down your shirt or pants until it melts.

- Go commando for the rest of the day.

- Sing the alphabet song backwards.

- Speak in at least three foreign accents for the next 15 minutes.

- Go on Facebook and change your relationship status every hour, for the entire day.

- Spell your name in the air using your butt!

- Perform a sexy dance, on the tune of a nursery rhyme like 'Twinkle Twinkle Little Star'.

- Ask for permission every time you need to use the bathroom the rest of the day.

- Act out a particular commercial ad.

- Do your partner's makeup.

- Make an obscene phone call to a friend (block your number - leave a message if they don't answer).

- Announce your love for your partner in public.

- Try to scratch your armpit with your big toe.

- Peel a banana with your feet.

- Eat a spoonful of hot sauce.

Word Scramble

Chose a side (right or left) to designate as your boxes. In your box, write down as many words as you can make from the letters each given phrase. Whomever comes up with the most words per phrase wins!

Agree on some rewards for the winner. Some ideas could be a picnic date, choice of the next movie you see, or a homemade dessert!

It was meant to be

Let's have a date night

I'm Crazy About You

Head Over Heels in Love

You're My Soulmate

Hangman

BASED ON THE GIVEN THEME, CREATE A GAME OF HANGMAN THAT YOUR PARTNER CAN COMPLETE!

Theme: Something about your first date

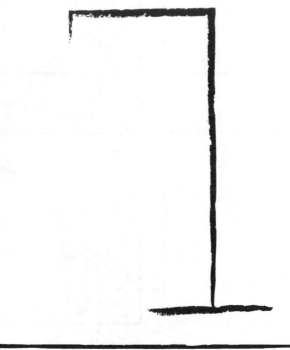

A B C D E F G H I J K L M
N O P Q R S T U V W X Y Z

Hangman

Based on the given theme, create a game of hangman that your partner can complete!

Theme: Your favorite memory together

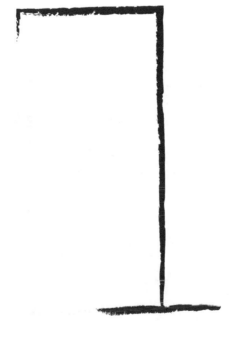

A   B   C   D   E   F   G   H   I   J   K   L   M

N   O   P   Q   R   S   T   U   V   W   X   Y   Z

Hangman

BASED ON THE GIVEN THEME, CREATE A GAME OF HANGMAN THAT YOUR PARTNER CAN COMPLETE!

Theme: Craziest time at a family function

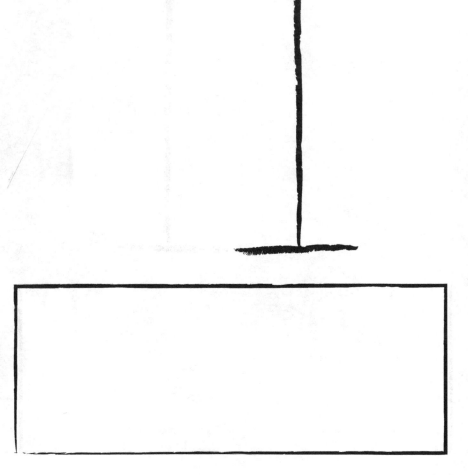

A B C D E F G H I J K L M
N O P Q R S T U V W X Y Z

Hangman

BASED ON THE GIVEN THEME, CREATE A GAME OF HANGMAN THAT YOUR PARTNER CAN COMPLETE!

Theme: Most memorable vacation spot

A   B   C   D   E   F   G   H   I   J   K   L   M
N   O   P   Q   R   S   T   U   V   W   X   Y   Z

I've Never...

Alternate turns and ask each other the following statements, then write your name in the appropriate spot following the statement. If you haven't done it, decide if it's something you'd like to try or not. Maybe the next time you can't think of something to do, you can refer to this nifty list!

I've never...been swimming with dolphins.

_____ has done this. _____ hasn't done this.

Is this something I want to try?   Heck yes!   - or -   No way Jose!

I've never...ran a marathon.

_____ has done this. _____ hasn't done this.

Is this something I want to try?   Heck yes!   - or -   No way Jose!

I've never...eaten sushi.

_____ has done this. _____ hasn't done this.

Is this something I want to try?   Heck yes!   - or -   No way Jose!

I've never...been to a wine tasting event.

_____ has done this. _____ hasn't done this.

Is this something I want to try?   Heck yes!   - or -   No way Jose!

I've never...had a spa weekend.

_____ has done this. _____ hasn't done this.

Is this something I want to try?   Heck yes!   - or -   No way Jose!

I've never...seen the sunrise in a natural setting.

_____ has done this. _____ hasn't done this.

Is this something I want to try?   Heck yes!   - or -   No way Jose!

I've never...been to a tail-gating party.

_____ HAS DONE THIS. _____ HASN'T DONE THIS.

IS THIS SOMETHING I WANT TO TRY?   HECK YES!   - OR -   NO WAY JOSE!

I've never...been on a hot-air balloon ride.

_____ HAS DONE THIS. _____ HASN'T DONE THIS.

IS THIS SOMETHING I WANT TO TRY?   HECK YES!   - OR -   NO WAY JOSE!

I've never...been to a small venue concert.

_____ HAS DONE THIS. _____ HASN'T DONE THIS.

IS THIS SOMETHING I WANT TO TRY?   HECK YES!   - OR -   NO WAY JOSE!

I've never...grown a vegetable garden.

_____ HAS DONE THIS. _____ HASN'T DONE THIS.

IS THIS SOMETHING I WANT TO TRY?   HECK YES!   - OR -   NO WAY JOSE!

I've never...travelled outside the country.

_____ HAS DONE THIS. _____ HASN'T DONE THIS.

IS THIS SOMETHING I WANT TO TRY?   HECK YES!   - OR -   NO WAY JOSE!

I've never...tried white water rafting.

_____ HAS DONE THIS. _____ HASN'T DONE THIS.

IS THIS SOMETHING I WANT TO TRY?   HECK YES!   – OR –   NO WAY JOSE!

I've never...learned to speak another language.

_____ HAS DONE THIS. _____ HASN'T DONE THIS.

IS THIS SOMETHING I WANT TO TRY?   HECK YES!   – OR –   NO WAY JOSE!

I've never...travelled somewhere by train.

_____ HAS DONE THIS. _____ HASN'T DONE THIS.

IS THIS SOMETHING I WANT TO TRY?   HECK YES!   – OR –   NO WAY JOSE!

I've never...volunteered for a charity or event.

_____ HAS DONE THIS. _____ HASN'T DONE THIS.

IS THIS SOMETHING I WANT TO TRY?   HECK YES!   – OR –   NO WAY JOSE!

I've never...ridden a horse.

_____ HAS DONE THIS. _____ HASN'T DONE THIS.

IS THIS SOMETHING I WANT TO TRY?   HECK YES!   – OR –   NO WAY JOSE!

I've never...taken a class for fun.

_____ HAS DONE THIS. _____ HASN'T DONE THIS.

IS THIS SOMETHING I WANT TO TRY?   HECK YES!   – OR –   NO WAY JOSE!

I've never...sang "The Devil Went Down to Georgia" at karaoke.

_____ HAS DONE THIS. _____ HASN'T DONE THIS.

IS THIS SOMETHING I WANT TO TRY?   HECK YES!   – OR –   NO WAY JOSE!

Picture This

EACH OF YOU GRAB A PIECE OF PAPER. SIT BACK TO BACK SO YOU CAN'T SEE YOUR PARTNER'S PAPER. ONE OF YOU WILL START DESCRIBING AN OBJECT (WITHOUT SAYING WHAT IT IS) WHILE THE OTHER PERSON DRAWS IT. (EX. IF YOU DESCRIBE A SNOWMAN, YOU MIGHT SAY "TOWARD THE BOTTOM OF THE PAPER, DRAW A CIRCLE. THEN DRAW A SMALLER CIRCLE ON TOP OF THAT, THEN A SMALLER CIRCLE ON TOP OF THAT ONE, ETC.) ONCE THE DESCRIPTION IS COMPLETE, THE ARTIST WILL SHOW THEIR DRAWING. SWITCH ROLES AND CONTINUE PLAYING UNTIL SOMEONE WINS BEST OUT OF THREE, OR UNTIL YOU'RE TIRED OF THE GAME AND JUST WANT TO GO GET ICE CREAM.

SCORING: IF THE DRAWING IS SPOT ON, THE ARTIST GETS ONE POINT AND THE PERSON DESCRIBING GETS TWO. IF IT LOOKS NOTHING LIKE THE DESCRIPTION, THE ARTIST GETS ONE POINT AND THE DESCRIBER GETS NONE.

Here are some ideas for things to draw:

- Snowmen having a snowball fight

- Birds flying south for the winter

- A city skyline at dusk

- A cowboy hat

- Ants at a picnic

- An open book

- A stick man or woman

- A baseball

99

How Would I Handle It?

Listed below are some fun, silly, and just ridiculous made-up scenarios. Imagine that they happened to you and your partner, and verbally describe how you think your partner would handle it!

...if we were attacked by zombies

...if cats ruled the world

...if I could live forever

...if one of us became famous

...if stores stopped selling my favorite snack/coffee/beer/etc.

...if our country was attacked by Godzilla's estranged son

...if I was an extra in a movie that starred my favorite actor

...if we were stranded on a desert island

...if we were stranded on a dessert island

...if I could fly

...if I could choose to veto one law

...if we had to spend an entire Saturday shopping at Ikea®

...if we could read minds

...if I became a greeting card writer

...if I could choose to have one superpower for a day

...if I had to chaperone a middle school dance

...if we could go anywhere in the world for a week for free

...if I could make all the world's major decisions for one day

...if my parents moved in with us

...if inanimate objects started talking

...if we switched bodies for one day

...if we became instant millionaires

Start a Conversation

HAVE NO MORE AWKWARD LAPSES IN CONVERSATION! HERE ARE 20 GREAT CONVERSATION STARTERS YOU CAN USE WHEN OUT ON A DATE, INSTEAD OF WATCHING TV, OR JUST WHEN YOU FEEL LIKE TALKING ABOUT SOMETHING NEW.

1. How many days could you last in solitary confinement?

2. What are some of your short-term goals?

3. What animal, besides humans, do you think would make the best world leaders?

4. Describe the best night of your teenage life.

5. If you had a million dollars that you had to give to charitable causes, how would you spend it?

6. Do you have any weird crushes on famous people that don't make sense to you?

7. What did you think was "cool" when you were around 8 years old?

8. How would you pitch a reality show about yourself?

9. Do you think your name suits you? What might be better?

10. If you could take a pill that made you never have a negative thought again, would you?

11. If you could have lived in a different decade, which one would it have been?

12. If you could have witnessed any biblical event, which one would you choose?

13. In your opinion, what makes a great parent?

14. What can we do as a couple to change the world in which we live?

15. If someone gave you enough money to start a business of your own, what kind of business would you start?

16. When making decisions, do you put more trust in facts or in feelings? Are you pleased with most of your decisions?

17. What are some of your long-term goals?

18. What would you most like people to remember you for after you die?

19. If you could bring any former leader from the past back to run our country today, who would it be?

20. Which one of the world's cultures do you find the most interesting and fascinating?

21. Describe something that's happened to you for which you have no explanation.

Find It...

Below is a list of the things you have to find on the next page. Starting at the same time and going in order, search for each item listed. When you find it, yell out "La-cucaracha!" and gameplay must stop. Write your initials next to the item you found then continue playing together. Whoever finds the most items by the end wins!

Things to find: Initials:

1. A penguin in a top hat   _____

2. A couple kissing   _____

3. A businessman on a cell phone   _____

4. A cooked turkey   _____

5. A ballet dancer   _____

6. A bald man eating ice cream   _____

7. The Statue of Liberty   _____

8. A St. Bernard with a barrel on its neck   _____

9. A baby holding a chicken   _____

10. A girl on a motorcycle   _____

11. A pair of cowboy boots (not together!)   _____

12. A lion with a mouse friend   _____

13. An open envelope   _____

14. A love note   _____

15. Two men wearing the same hat   _____

16. A woman singing   _____

17. A monster eating a sandwich   _____

18. King Kong on the Eiffel Tower   _____

19. A pair of scissors   _____

20. A couple of pandas holding hands   _____

Comic Strip Creators

FEATURING YOU AND YOUR HONEY, COMPLETE THESE COMICS BY ADDING FACES, COSTUMES AND DIALOGUE. IN THE LAST BOX, CREATE AN AWESOME ENDING USING YOUR OWN OUTSTANDING CREATIVITY!

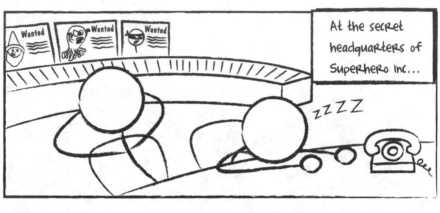

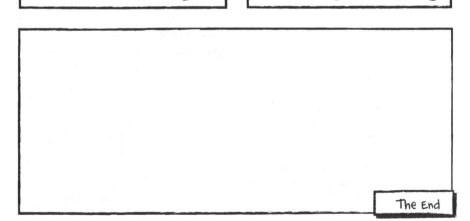

Comic Strip Creators

FEATURING YOU AND YOUR HONEY, COMPLETE THESE COMICS BY ADDING FACES AND DIALOGUE. IN THE LAST BOX, CREATE AN AWESOME ENDING USING YOUR OWN OUTSTANDING CREATIVITY!

109

Who Can Do It First?

This game tests your ability to make you and your partner look ridiculous. Using the ideas below, plus any that you can come up with, compete to see who can finish them first. This is a great game to play during dinner, while waiting for a movie, or even just while taking a stroll down the block.

- Make a waiter say the word "Worcestershire".

- Get a stranger to laugh (a real one, not a courtesy laugh).

- Convince a family member that you're moving out of the country.

- Randomly make the other believe a ridiculous made-up "fact".

- Do a handstand in an outdoor downtown area.

- Give a standing ovation at the end of a movie (in the theatre).

- Pull off a convincing foreign accent in public.

- Balance empty cans on your head until the tower falls.

Come up with some of your own!

_____

_____

_____

_____

_____

_____

Verbal Tennis

On of you will say a word, and your partner must respond with the first word that comes to their mind, then you'll reply with another word, and so on. The round ends when no more relevant words can be stated. This is a great way to get to know each other through simple dialogue! See how long you can keep it up!

Possible starter words:

- A place you'd love to visit

- An area you might want to live in someday

- A type of pet you would like to have

- Your favorite name for a child

- A future dream that you both may share

- Something that you'd like to experience together

- A secret dream that you've never told the other about

- One adjective describing how you feel about the other person

Crossword Puzzle

GRAB YOUR HONEY AND FILL OUT THIS CROSSWORD PUZZLE TOGETHER!

ROMANTIC PICNIC

Across:

2. Two-Pointer

4. Ketchup, mustard, e.g.

6. Get lovey-dovey

7. Gentle wind

10. Hill builders

14. They sit on laps

16. Classic Wham-O toy

17. Lucky Charms

18. In the open air

Down:

1. Patio appliance

3. Isolated

5. School vacation time

8. Take it easy

9. Gearshift position

11. B.L.T., e.g.

12. Chianti or Chablis

13. Checkered spread

15. Fruit with a green rind

(ANSWERS ON PAGE 121)

What Does it Say?

Imagine your friend wants to set you up with someone, and the only thing you know about them is their favorite movies, TV shows or songs. What would you think about them?

Both of you will write down five of your favorites for each of the given categories. Once you finish, read your items aloud to your partner. Assuming this is the only information given about you, your sweetie has to tell you one adjective (per category) they think best describes you based on your lists. If you don't have anything to list in a category, change it to something that suits you better. Get to know each other once again!

TV Shows (Look on: Hulu, Netflix, DVDs, Favorites, DVR list)

Player One:

Player Two:

_____   _____

_____   _____

_____   _____

_____   _____

_____   _____

Adjective:

Adjective:

_____   _____

Movies (Look at: DVDs, iTunes, Favorites)

Player One:

Player Two:

_____   _____

_____   _____

_____   _____

_____   _____

_____

Adjective:

_____

Books (Look at: E-Readers, Bookshelves, Favorites)

Player One: Player Two:

_____   _____

_____   _____

_____   _____

_____   _____

_____   _____

Adjective: Adjective:

_____   _____

Drinks (Look in: Fridge, Pantry, Liquor Cabinet, Wine Rack)

Player One: Player Two:

_____   _____

_____   _____

_____   _____

_____   _____

_____   _____

Adjective: Adjective:

_____   _____

Home Decor (Look at: Paint Colors, Furniture style, Cleanliness)

Player One:

_____

_____

_____

_____

_____

Adjective:

_____

Player Two:

_____

_____

_____

_____

_____

Adjective:

_____

Clothing (Look at: Style, Accessories, Shoes)

Player One:

_____

_____

_____

_____

_____

Adjective:

_____

Player Two:

_____

_____

_____

_____

_____

Adjective:

_____

School (Look at: College courses, Favorite subjects, Interests)

Player One:

_____

_____

_____

Player Two:

_____

_____

_____

_____

_____

Adjective:

_____

Beauty Products (Look at: Hair products, Makeup, Styling tools)

Player One: Player Two:

_____   _____

_____   _____

_____   _____

_____   _____

_____   _____

Adjective: Adjective:

_____   _____

Magazines (Look at: E-Readers, Subscriptions, Favorites)

Player One: Player Two:

_____   _____

_____   _____

_____   _____

_____   _____

_____   _____

Adjective: Adjective:

_____   _____

Mind Map of Life

We've given you starting points in the bubbles, now you can fill in the additions based on what you and your partner want out of life. It's like talking about your future, visually!

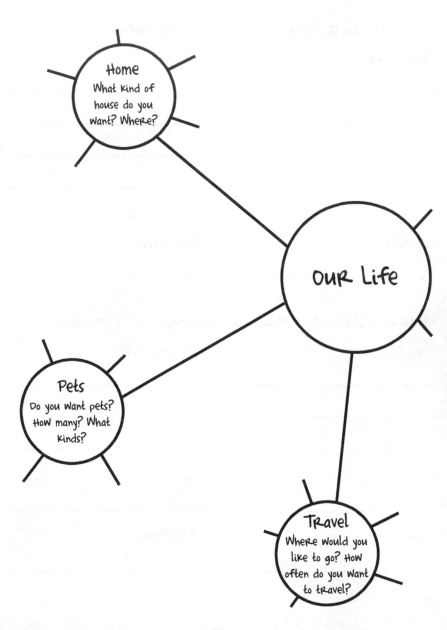

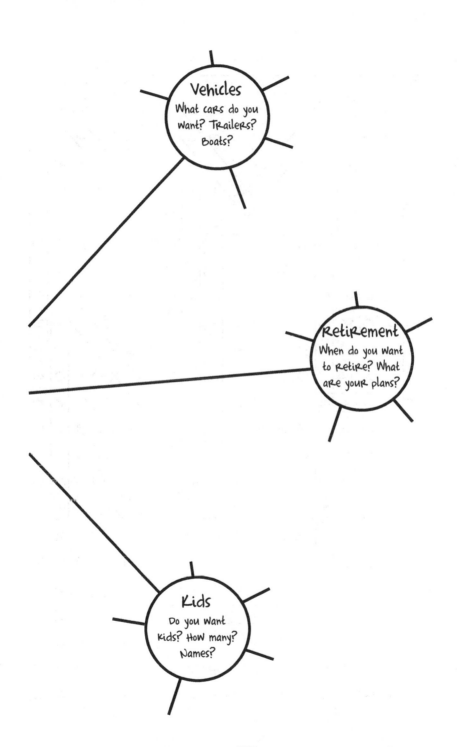

Vehicles
What cars do you
want? Trailers?
Boats?

Retirement
When do you want
to retire? What
are your plans?

Kids
Do you want
kids? How many?
Names?

Word Search Answers:

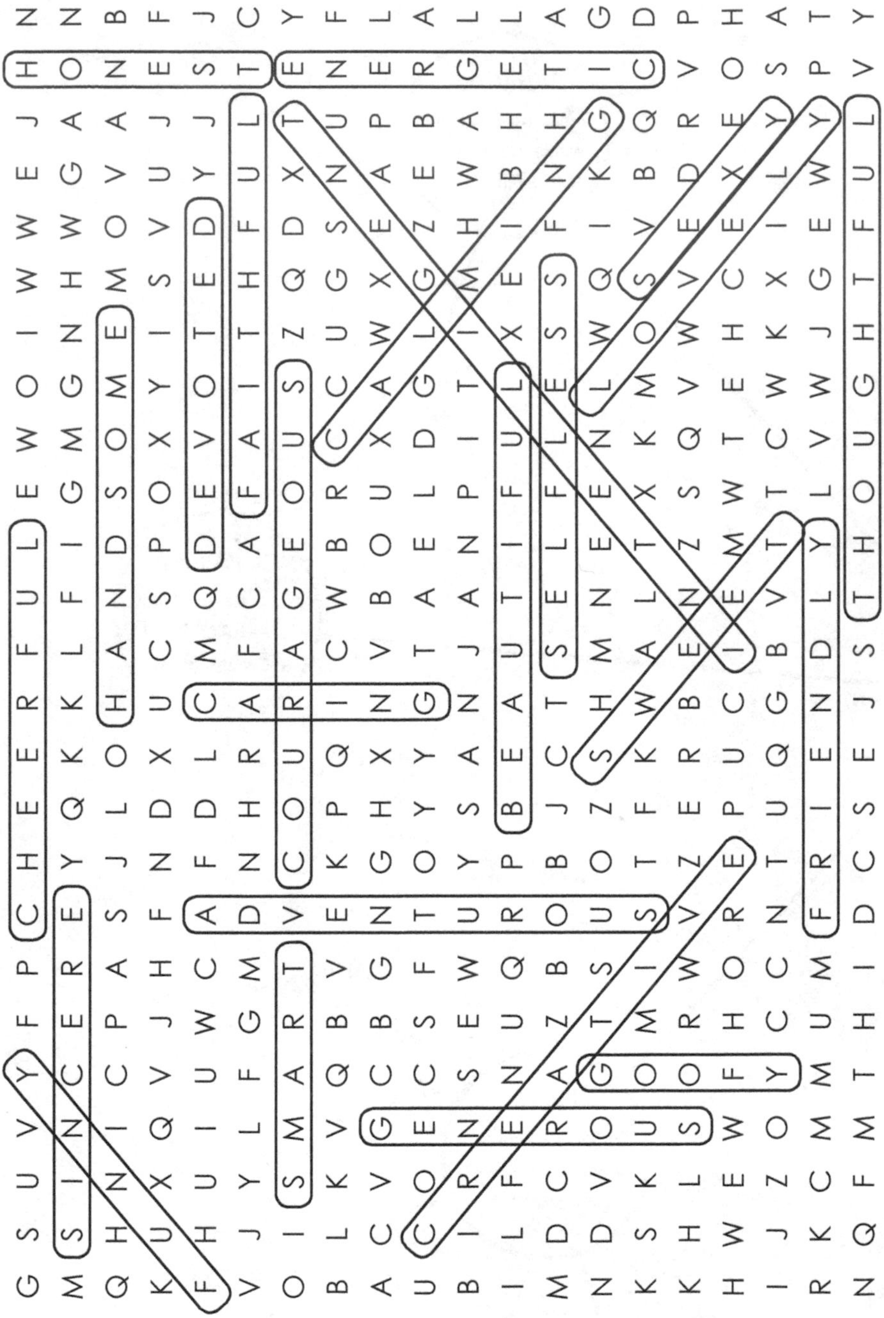

CROSSWORD PUZZLE ANSWERS:

About
LoveBook™

We are a group of individuals who
want to spread love in all its forms. We
believe love fuels the world and every
relationship is important. We hope this
book helps build on that belief.

www.LoveBookOnline.com

CPSIA information can be obtained
at www.ICGtesting.com
Printed in the USA
BVHW080247081219
565980BV00001B/97/P